# CITY IN TIME | Boston

# CITY IN TIME | Boston

## JEFFREY HANTOVER

### ORIGINAL PHOTOGRAPHY BY GILBERT KING

STERLING

New York / London
www.sterlingpublishing.com

STERLING and the distinctive Sterling logo are registered trademarks of Sterling Publishing Co., Inc.

Library of Congress Cataloging-in-Publication Data Available

2  4  6  8  10  9  7  5  3  1

Published by Sterling Publishing Co., Inc.
387 Park Avenue South, New York, NY 10016
© 2008 by Sterling Publishing Co., Inc.

Distributed in Canada by Sterling Publishing
*c/o* Canadian Manda Group, 165 Dufferin Street
Toronto, Ontario, Canada M6K 3H6
Distributed in the United Kingdom by GMC Distribution Services
Castle Place, 166 High Street, Lewes, East Sussex, England BN7 1XU
Distributed in Australia by Capricorn Link (Australia) Pty. Ltd.
P.O. Box 704, Windsor, NSW 2756, Australia

*Printed in China*

Many of the archival photographs featured in the *City in Time* series are more than 100 years old
and have not been altered to conceal damage or wear from the effects of time.

Sterling ISBN-13: 978-1-4027-3300-0
          ISBN-10: 1-4027-3300-3

For information about custom editions, special sales, premium and
corporate purchases, please contact Sterling Special Sales
Department at 800-805-5489 or specialsales@sterlingpublishing.com.

# *Preface*

**W**e hope that this volume of the *City in Time* series will compel you first to wonder at, then appreciate, and ultimately better understand the development and achievements of the world's great urban centers. The series not only offers interesting time-lapsed juxtapositions, but also meaningfully contrasting images, shedding light on the unique resources, circumstances, and creative forces that propelled these cities to greatness. In a world where renovation and development are so often casually destructive, visual history can be a reservoir of wisdom from which we can inspire and refresh ourselves. We invite you to reflect upon the accomplishments of those who came before us and revel in these impressive monuments to human ambition.

# Introduction

*If time travel is ever realized, it will likely be done in a lab at MIT or Harvard. In the meantime, Boston invites anyone with a good pair of shoes to travel back and forth through almost four centuries in a day. It is striking that when Bostonians speak of the pleasures of their city, they most often grow rhapsodic over walking around the city. It is a city of discovery, of delights found around a corner, blossoming in parks and gardens, or stumbled upon in neighborhoods that both surprise with change and comfort with constancy. Los Angeles is best seen from a helicopter, Chicago from a car traveling along Lake Shore Drive between the lake and the Loop, and New York from a double-deck tour bus going down Fifth Avenue. Boston, on the other hand, is best appreciated on foot, so as to savor its still-human scale, its distinctive neighborhoods, and our national history, visible in brick and granite.*

Boston is a city layered in history and change—more layered than the cream pie that bears its name. I.M. Pei and Philip Johnson share the stage with Bulfinch, Richardson, and McKim, Mead and White; Swan Boats with bronze ducklings; and Revolutionary patriots with champion Patriots.

History in Boston is immediate and concrete. You can stand in churches and meeting houses where patriots assailed British rule and abolitionists called for the end of slavery. You can pass classrooms where Nobel laureates wrote equations on blackboards and houses where early nineteenth-century writers shaped the country's culture, or stroll through the Common, where citizens like yourself took their leisure. Though much of the architectural past was consumed in the fires of the nineteenth century or destroyed by man's good intentions in the twentieth, much still remains, as the photos in this book evidence. Many of these survivors are living presences—churches with full Sunday services, squares with townhouses alight on Christmas Eve, and revitalized markets full of shoppers with full stomachs.

Boston has survived and surmounted the population decline of the mid-twentieth century, the destruction of neighborhoods and the urban social fabric by the Central Artery, the concrete sterility of Government Center, and the racial strife of the 1970s. The Central Artery is a buried memory and the Big Dig as much a celebration of park design as tunnel construction. The writer Susan Orlean returned to the city a few years ago to find it "younger, more agile, and refreshed." Perhaps in some paradoxical way, the city has become younger by embracing, not embalming, its past. If all is paved over or leached from life, then the homogeneity of the new oppresses rather than refreshes. Boston is that special mix of past and present that instills hope in the future.

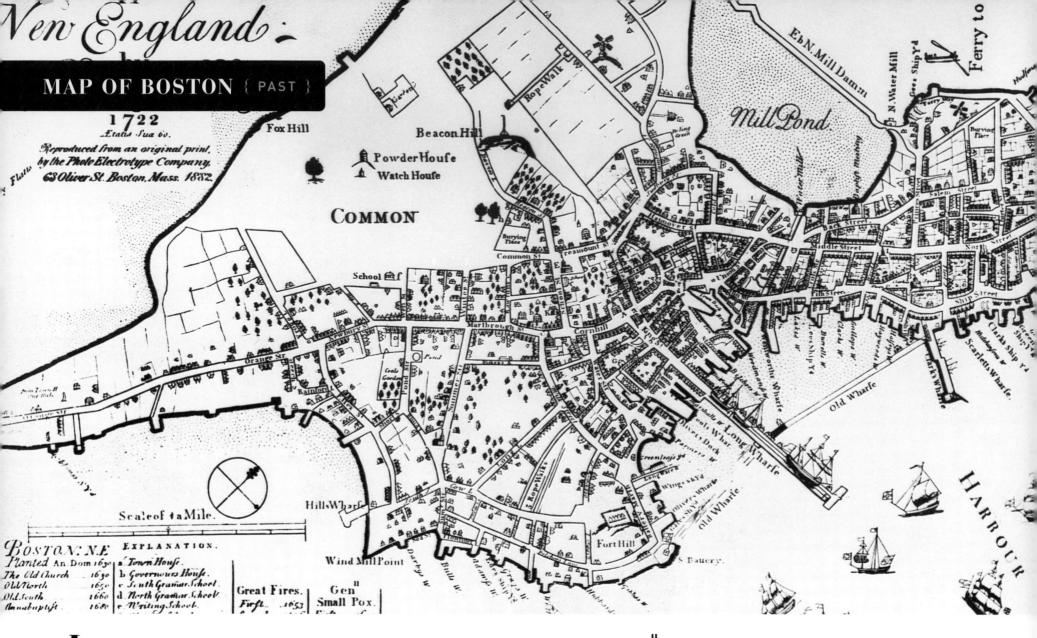

In 1630, when Boston got its name, the city was "a tiny tadpole of land, the Shawmut Peninsula, that clung by its tail to a vast unknown continent." If a Boston map from that era were imposed on a modern map, it would cover less than half of the present-day city. Between 1630 and 1890, the physical size of the city tripled as the marshes, mud flats, and spaces between the wharves along the waterfront were filled in. From 1857 to 1894, trains laden with landfill traveled every forty-five minutes around the clock to build up the 580 acres of Back Bay.

O nto this expanded landmass came large numbers of immigrants from Ireland, Italy, and the shtetls of Eastern Europe, and later, African-American migrants from the deep South. Today, Boston covers only 48.4 square miles with a population of nearly 600,000, making it the third smallest American city in area with a population over 500,000, after Washington, D.C. and San Francisco. However, on a typical day you'd find nearly twice as many people in the city working, shopping, studying, or sightseeing.

The 45 acres purchased from Reverend William Blackstone in 1634 are now the oldest urban park in America. Here Colonial Bostonians pastured their cattle (until 1830), exercised their horses, fought duels, drilled their militias, and hung unrepentant Quakers. In 1836, the old wooden pasture fences were removed and footpaths were laid down—the Long Path from Joy Street to the corner of Boylston and Tremont Streets is the most famous. During the Victorian era, the paths were straightened and some were paved.

**T**he Common remains the green heart of Boston, site of intimate encounters and mass celebrations. Thousands heard Martin Luther King Jr., Pope John Paul II, and Billy Graham speak here, and Judy Garland entertained over 100,000 in 1967. Today, as in the past, Bostonians stroll down the malls laid out first along Beacon, Park, and Tremont Streets and later, Charles and Boylston. They glide on the Frog Pond skating rink, which was built in 1997, and listen to music in the restored Parkman Bandstand.

Augustus Saint-Gaudens's high relief bronze sculpture commemorates the sacrifice of Colonel Robert Gould Shaw, son of a privileged abolitionist family, and the Fifty-fourth Regiment of Massachusetts Volunteer Infantry, the first black regiment recruited in the North. Shaw and his men died during the unsuccessful assault on Fort Wagner in 1863. The monument was erected through a fund established by Joshua B. Smith, a fugitive slave, former employee of the Shaw family, and state representative. Booker T. Washington was among the speakers at the dedication on May 31, 1897.

## ROBERT GOULD SHAW AND THE MASSACHUSETTS FIFTY-FOURTH REGIMENT MEMORIAL { PRESENT }

The memorial is now the first of fourteen stops on the Black Heritage Trail. Originally it bore only the names of the slain white officers, and it wasn't until 1984 that the names of the sixty-two black infantrymen who died were added. All were memorialized in the 1989 film *Glory*, which featured Denzel Washington and Morgan Freeman, and starred Matthew Broderick as Shaw, "the blue-eyed child of fortune" whom William James had praised at the monument's dedication.

Charles Bulfinch, fresh from touring Europe, drew up a plan for a new Massachusetts State House when he was only twenty-four. On July 4, 1795, Governor Samuel Adams, helped by Paul Revere and others, laid the cornerstone atop Beacon Hill on pasture land once owned by the state's first governor, John Hancock. The State House was completed in 1798.

## LORE & LEGEND

The State House's distinctive dome—even more so than that of the national capitol, which was also designed by Bulfinch—inspired the domes that have become an almost universal feature of other American state houses.

The State House has grown as the state government has grown, but its additions have tried to stay true to Bulfinch's original design and redbrick structure, though the building, like its politicians, changed colors often. The redbrick was painted white in 1825, yellow-gold in 1855, white again during WWI, and back to the original redbrick in 1928. The dome, first made of wood, then sheathed in copper by Paul Revere in 1802 to prevent leaking, did not get its 23-karat gold leaf until 1874.

**B**uilt on 24 acres of reclaimed marshland, the Public Garden is the refined neighbor of the Common. After a failed private conservatory and botanic garden, and misguided efforts to subdivide the land for house lots, a public competition in 1859 awarded a one-hundred-dollar prize to George Meacham's formal landscape design. Two years later, a three-acre pond with a miniature island was added. In 1877, the Swan Boats set sail.

## LORE & LEGEND

The designer of the Swan Boats, Robert Paget, was inspired by the popularity of bicycles and Wagner's Lohengrin, whose knightly hero traveled by a swan-drawn boat.

**B**ostonians know spring has arrived when, in mid-April, the Swan Boats once more glide on the pond. Robert Paget's grandson Paul now commands a six-swan fleet. The original boats each carried eight single seats. The present boats are replicas with fiberglass instead of copper swans, and they carry up to twenty passengers seated on five or six benches during their fifteen-minute pedal-power cruises. An 1859 Act of the Massachusetts Legislature forever preserves the Public Garden as open space, so all the Swans need to survive are more Pagets and good weather.

The "discretely Art Deco" Ritz-Carlton, overlooking the Public Garden, opened in May 1927 as the first building to break the five-story skyline of Arlington Street. The hotel of choice for society, royalty, and celebrities, it was the first hotel in America to provide private baths in the rooms, white-tie-and-apron uniforms for waiters and waitresses, a black-tie uniform for the maître d', and morning suits for all other staff. Howard Hughes, Bette Davis, Shirley Temple, and Tennessee Williams, are among the many stars to have stayed here.

The first Ritz-Carlton in the United States and the only one to survive the Depression, the Ritz-Carlton Boston celebrated its seventy-fifth anniversary in 2002 with a major restoration. The original building remains, but without the name. The Taj group bought the hotel in 2007, and renamed it the Taj Boston. The Ritz-Carlton Boston Common on Avery Street now carries on the old name. When the Ritz opened in 1927, a suite was forty dollars—just enough for tea service in the Taj Lounge today.

Louisburg Square, one of the last areas of Beacon Hill to be developed, is a private square of Greek Revival townhouses built in the late 1830s and 40s surrounding an enclosed park. The Louisburg Square Proprietors, America's first homeowners' association, was established in 1844 to maintain the private park. In the nineteenth century, some of the city's literary lights lived here, including William Dean Howells at No. 4, and Bronson Alcott and his daughter Louisa May at No. 20.

The townhouses now have multi-million-dollar price tags, but Louisburg Square still has the same quiet charm it had in the mid-nineteenth century. Statues donated to the homeowners' association in 1850 by a Greek merchant who lived on the square stand silent guard: Columbus to the north and Aristides the Just, the Athenian statesman, to the south. Though many homes have been split up into condominiums and rental apartments, traditions persist. Windows still glow with candles, and carolers make their way around the square on Christmas Eve.

Built almost entirely by African-American artisans in 1806 for the First African Baptist Church, the African Meeting House is the oldest African-American church still standing in the United States. In 1800, the 1,100 free black Bostonians had no voting privileges in white churches and were forced to sit in their balconies. Known as the Black Faneuil Hall, the Meeting House was a center for the African-American community and a forum for abolitionist activity. William Lloyd Garrison helped found the New England Anti-Slavery Society here in 1832.

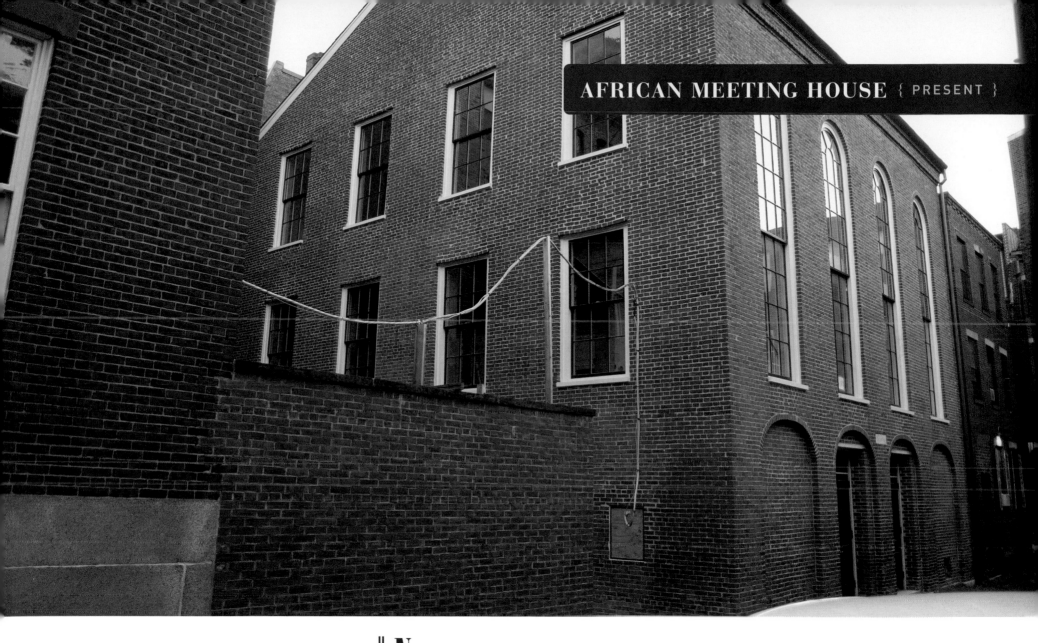

Near the end of the nineteenth century, the African-American community began to migrate from the West End to the South End and Roxbury, and the building was sold to a Jewish congregation. It served as a synagogue until it was acquired by the Museum of African American History in 1972. The museum is now part of the Boston African American National Historic Site and the 1.6-mile Black Heritage Trail, which give visitors a glimpse into the history of Boston's nineteenth-century African-American community.

Considered the city's first real concert hall, the Boston Music Hall opened in 1852. Jenny Lind sang here and Ralph Waldo Emerson and Booker T. Washington spoke from its stage. In 1863, a $60,000 German organ with 5,474 pipes was installed. The Boston Music Hall is best known as the first home of the Boston Symphony Orchestra, which performed here from 1881 until its move to Symphony Hall in 1900. In 1885, the ever-popular Boston Pops began here as Promenade Concerts.

The Music Hall's famous organ is now a part of the Methuen Memorial Music Hall in Methuen, Massachusetts, and the space—renamed the Orpheum Theatre—has moved over the years from hosting vaudeville to movies to rock concerts. Once praised for its opulent interior with busts of classical composers and a copy of the Apollo Belvedere, the theatre now receives mixed reviews. Some rock concertgoers call it a hidden jewel with fine acoustics, while others complain of torn seats, a terrible sound system, and an overall decrepit condition.

Since 1809, the 217-foot steeple of the Park Street Church has been a visible Boston landmark. The church was founded primarily by Congregationalist members of the Old South Church who, according to the church's present-day Web site, were disturbed by "increasing apostasy from the gospel and rising Unitarianism in New England. It was a church of firsts: the first Sunday school in 1818; the first prison aid in 1824; William Lloyd Garrison's first public anti-slavery speech in 1829; and, in 1831, the first singing of "My Country 'Tis of Thee."

**P**ark Street Church remains an active, thriving Congregational church. It continues its nineteenth-century tradition of social involvement with ministries to the homeless and support of the educational needs of inner-city youth, among other activities. Though its pastor in 1897 denounced the subway being built next door as the work of the devil, the church now welcomes the many visitors it brings to this popular stop on the Freedom Trail.

# A City of "Firsts"

*As the nation's first major city, it is not surprising that Boston would be home to a long list of firsts, including these innovations:*

- The nations' first **CHOCOLATE MILL**, established by John Hannon in 1756.

- America's first **HUMAN FLIGHT** when John Childs jumped off the steeple of the Old North Church in 1757 in a feathered glider and flew 700 feet to the ground.

- The first American **RAILROAD—** Gridley Bryant's horse-drawn tram to move granite from his Quincy quarry in 1826.

- The first American-born **WOMAN TO SPEAK PUBLICLY** before an audience of men and women when Maria Stewart, an African-American writer and activist, gave her farewell address in 1833 in the school room of the African Meeting House.

- America's first **BALLROOM BUILT ON SPRINGS** at Papanti Dance Studio in Scollay Square in 1837.

- The first woman in America to be given **ANESTHESIA DURING CHILDBIRTH** (Longfellow's second wife, Fanny, in 1847).

- The country's first **AIR-CONDITIONING SYSTEM**, installed in 1848 at the old Boston Museum.

- America's first **AERIAL PHOTO** taken from a balloon in 1860.

- The printing of the first **CHRISTMAS CARD** in America in 1875.

- The first American **PERFORMANCE OF HANDEL'S MESSIAH** in 1876 in King's Chapel.

- The first **SUBWAY LINE** in America in 1897.

- Gillette and Nickerson's invention of the first **DISPOSABLE RAZOR BLADE** in 1901.

- The first **OIL PAINTING BY MATISSE** to enter an American collection in 1911 at the Isabella Stewart Gardener Museum.

- The first **E-MAIL MESSAGE** in the world sent in 1971 at the Cambridge firm of Bolt, Beranek, and Newman.

- The first **COMPUTER SPREADSHEET PROGRAM**, conceived in 1978 by a Harvard MBA student, Dan Bricklin.

The South Burying Ground, founded in 1660 from part of the Boston Common, got its present name in 1737 when the town granary moved to the adjacent site now occupied by the Park Street Church. It is best known for the Revolutionary War heroes buried here, including three signers of the Declaration of Independence, the victims of the Boston Massacre, and Paul Revere, among others.

## LORE & LEGEND

Simon Willard, designer of the Bunker Hill Monument, designed the granite obelisk commemorating Benjamin Franklin's parents.

Burials in the Granary Burying Ground stopped in 1880. An estimated 5,000 (though some say as many as 12,000) bodies were randomly buried, often one atop the other, under 2,345 gravestones and crowded into 137 tombs. Landscaping projects in the 1830s tried to make the Granary Burying Ground more inviting for the living. Gravestones clustered in the center were rearranged into neat rows, shade trees and shrubbery were planted, and paths were laid out. Over the last twenty years, the Granary has undergone restoration and improvement as part of a citywide Historic Burying Ground Initiative.

Founded in 1807, the Boston Athenaeum is one of the country's oldest independent libraries. Overlooking the Granary Burying Ground and modeled after a Palladian palazzo in Vicenza, the present building was completed in 1849. With sculpture and painting galleries, it was the city's first museum of fine arts, and its collection became the nucleus of the newly formed Museum of Fine Arts. Among its major early holdings were the King's Chapel Collection, sent by King William III in 1698, and most of George Washington's private library, purchased in 1848.

## LORE & LEGEND

The Boston Athenaeum's extension at 14 Beacon Street served as the exterior for the law offices of Cage, Fish, and Associates on television's *Ally McBeal*.

In 1914, the building was renovated and its fourth and fifth floors were added. Currently the library has more than a half million volumes. Among its strengths are Boston and New England history, English and American literature, and the fine and decorative arts. Its special collections include early works in Native American languages and imprints of the Confederate States, along with first editions by Lord Byron and T.S. Eliot.

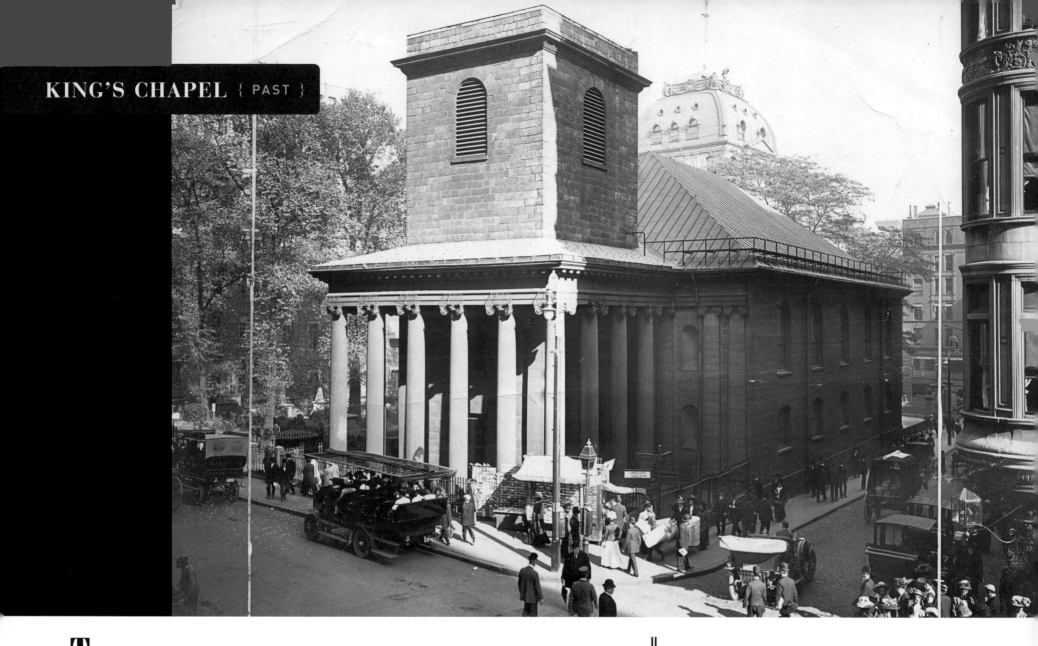

The original King's Chapel, the first Anglican church in New England, was built in 1688 on land seized by the governor from the city's burying ground because no resident would sell land for a non-Puritan church. The current structure, completed in 1754, was the first large building in the colonies built of quarried stone, but limited funds dictated the truncated half steeple and wooden, faux-stone columns. Under the leadership of James Freeman, who revised the Book of Common Prayer, it became the first Unitarian church in America in 1785.

K ing's Chapel is the fifth stop along the Freedom Trail. A bell forged in England was hung in the church in 1772. It cracked in 1814 and was recast by Paul Revere who claimed it was "the sweetest bell I ever made." The bell continues to be rung at the church's Sunday service. Despite his changes to the liturgy, Freeman considered King's Chapel to be Anglican, but the Anglican bishop refused to ordain him. Today, the church still follows its own mixed Anglican and Unitarian liturgy.

The Parker House, opened in 1855, is the country's oldest continuously operating hotel. Harvey Parker greeted his guests personally, introduced the European Plan (which separated food and lodging charges), initiated the practice of serving food continuously, and coined the term "scrod" for the fresh whitefish catch of the day. Members of the Saturday Club—literary elite and politicos such as Emerson, Lowell, Longfellow, and Whittier—met here monthly. The most infamous nineteenth-century guest was John Wilkes Booth, who was practicing pistol shooting nearby and stayed here before leaving to assassinate Lincoln.

## LORE & LEGEND

The hotel's staff is also notable: Vietnamese leader Ho Chi Minh worked here as a baker and Malcolm X was once a bus boy.

The current fifteen-story hotel replaced the original building in 1927. Now part of the Omni chain, the hotel underwent an $80 million renovation in 2000, and an inspection of the facade in 2007. The city's only rooftop ballroom remains, and Parker House rolls and Boston Cream Pie are still on the menu. It was here that JFK announced his first Congressional candidacy in 1946 and proposed to Jackie.

B uilt between 1862 and 1865 on the site of both the Boston Latin School (the first public school in America) and, later, the Suffolk County Courthouse, the Old City Hall was one of the first American buildings in the French Second Empire style of the Tuileries Palace and the Louvre. The Executive Office Building in D.C. and city halls in Baltimore, Philadelphia, and Providence were also built in this popular style, sometimes called the General Grant style. Statues of Benjamin Franklin and Mayor Josiah Quincy flank the entrance.

**O**nce called "a lunatic pile of a building; a great, grim, resolutely ugly dustcatcher" by Edwin O'Connor in *The Last Hurrah*, the Old City Hall is now an award-winning example of historic preservation and adaptive reuse that stimulated the repurposing of landmark buildings nationally in the 1970s and 80s. Between 1969 and 1971, after winning a public competition, the Architectural Heritage Foundation gutted the interior while keeping the exterior intact. The building now houses a mix of corporate and non-profit tenants and an upscale steak restaurant.

A section of interlocking streets, Scollay Square was officially named in 1838 for a building bought by William Scollay forty-three years earlier at the intersection of Cambridge and Court Streets. The square is best remembered for its decline from an elite residential area in the early nineteenth century to a commercial center with restaurants, bars, and vaudeville theatres, and then home to burlesque houses, shooting galleries, and tattoo parlors. Scollay Square ended as a sleazy magnet for sailors on leave and Harvard men in search of extracurricular education.

As early as the 1930s, there were proposals for a new government center in Scollay Square. What the Depression and WWII delayed finally became a reality in 1962, when Scollay Square was bulldozed—1000 buildings were demolished and 20,000 residents displaced—to begin work on Government Center. The center's keystone is the new Boston City Hall, which one architectural critic called a "grim chunk of concrete." With the exception of occasional celebrations to honor the region's championship sports teams, the vast City Hall Plaza is a lifeless expanse, far from the human tumult of Scollay Square.

The Old State House, Boston's oldest surviving public building, was built in 1713 and was home to the Royal Governor's Council Chamber and the Massachusetts Assembly. It was here that John Adams heard James Otis's fiery words against the Writs of Assistance; he later claimed that "Then and there, the child Independence was born." The Boston Massacre took place in front of its stately doors and the Declaration of Independence was first read to Bostonians from the balcony. The building served as the State House until 1798 and as the City Hall from 1830 to 1841.

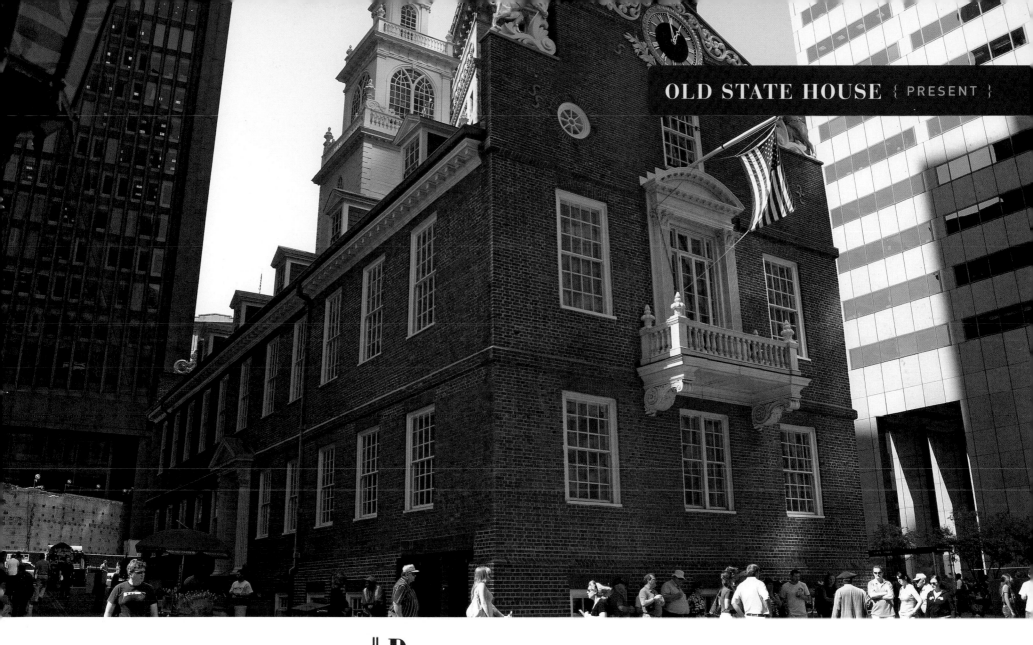

Returned to commercial use in 1841, the building eventually fell into disrepair. Incensed by Chicago's offer to move it for the World's Fair, a citizen's group spearheaded the 1882 restoration. The Old State House is now a museum operated by the Bostonian Society. As of this writing, the building, damaged by storms and nor'easters, is again threatened. Because of cuts in the National Park Service budget, the Bostonian Society needs to raise significant funds for repairs to prevent permanent loss or structural failure.

This gambrel-roofed structure, built in 1712 as an apothecary and residence, was a center of nineteenth-century publishing and literary activity. For seventy-four years, starting in 1829, booksellers occupied this space. The most famous was Ticknor & Fields, the nation's leading publisher at the time who, from 1833 to 1864, published the works of Longfellow, Hawthorne, Emerson, John Greenleaf Whittier, Dickens, Oliver Wendell Holmes, and Louisa May Alcott—many of whom were founders and contributors to the *Atlantic Monthly* magazine, headquartered here.

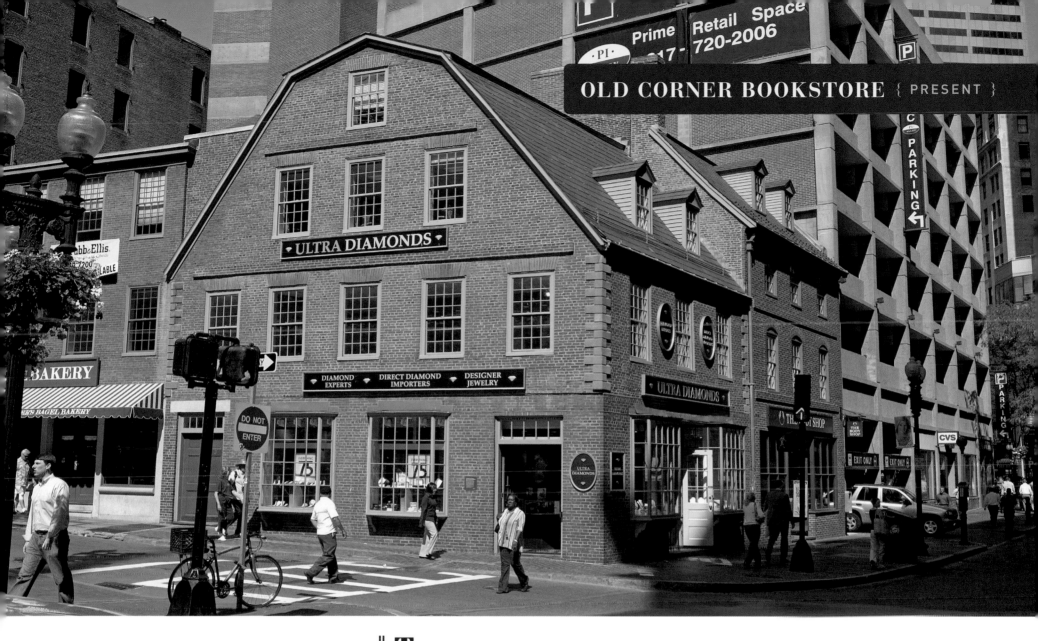

The last bookseller moved out in 1903, and by the 1950s the building was a pizza parlor slated to be torn down to make way for a parking garage. With support from the *Boston Globe*, Historic Boston Incorporated bought the site and raised private donations to extensively restore the interior and exterior of the building over the next two decades. In addition to being a stop on the Freedom Trail and Literary Trail, the Old Corner Bookstore is the name of a real estate endowment that supports architectural preservation in the city.

# Literary Boston

From Longfellow to Love Story, *and from Hawthorne to Stephen King, the streets of Boston and its environs are paved with literary history. One doesn't have to travel far to find a site of literary inspiration, a meeting place of literary minds, or an author's final resting place. Here are a few:*

- **THE PUBLIC GARDEN'S POND AND ISLAND,** where Mrs. Mallard and her eight ducklings found a home in Robert McCloskey's award-winning children's book, *Make Way for Ducklings* and were immortalized in bronze by artist Nancy Schön.

- **THE SUITE AT THE RITZ-CARLTON** (now the Taj Boston) where Tennessee Williams revised *A Streetcar Named Desire*.

- **THE HARVARD MEDICAL SCHOOL,** where Fannie Farmer, whose cookbook outsold the popular novels of her day, once taught nutrition.

- **THE ANDERSON MEMORIAL BRIDGE** over the Charles River, where a plaque commemorates William Faulkner's fictional freshman, Quentin Compson, who in *The Sound and the Fury* jumped to his death from the earlier bridge that once spanned the river.

- **FORT INDEPENDENCE ON CASTLE ISLAND,** where Edgar Allen Poe was stationed and which became inspiration for the entombed officer in "The Cask of Amontillado."

- **SEASON TICKET-HOLDER STEPHEN KING'S SEAT AT FENWAY PARK,** where he watched the miraculous season of 2004, chronicled with Steward O'Nan in *Faithful: Two Diehard Boston Red Sox Fans Chronicle the Historic 2004 Season*.

- **THE HARVARD YARD,** where Jennifer Cavilleri and Oliver Barrett IV fell in love and learned never to say they were sorry in Eric Segal's Kleenex novel, *Love Story*.

Filene's Basement, built in 1912, is known less for being famed Chicago architect Daniel Burnham's last major building than for its "Automatic Bargain Basement," introduced in 1908 at its earlier location across the street. Initially, leftovers from the Filene's department store were dumped for sale at markdown prices, but soon the bargain store was buying leftover merchandise from other stores.

## LORE & LEGEND

In the early days, merchandise at Filene's Basement was tagged with its original date and sale price, and automatically discounted 25% after twelve days, 50% after eighteen days, 75% after twenty-four days, and given to charity after thirty days.

The flagship store of Filene's Basement (now a separately owned and operated company) was placed on the National Register of Historic Places in 1986. The company claims that the store is Boston's second most popular tourist attraction, drawing 15,000 to 20,000 shoppers daily. Urban legends abound of frantic female shoppers engaging in tug-of-wars and fisticuffs, stripping in the aisles to change, and hiding merchandise in hopes of later bargains.

Five thousand Bostonians rallied against the British tax on tea in this Puritan meetinghouse on December 16, 1773. Led by the Sons of Liberty disguised as Mohawks, a crowd went to Griffin's Wharf, and the American Revolution was born. Built in 1729, it was Boston's largest building at the time and held meetings Faneuil Hall was unable to accommodate. During the war, the British desecrated this symbol of rebellion, ripping out pews and turning it into a military riding school.

Even before the Great Fire of 1872, the congregation of the Old South Meeting House had decided to move to Copley Square. Its imminent demolition energized "twenty women of Boston" who, aided by Emerson, Longfellow, and others, led the first successful effort to save a public building for its historical value. The building has been a museum since 1877. Known for its educational programs and its commitment to free speech, it is also famous for its annual reenactment of the Boston Tea Party, with free admission for spectators in colonial costume.

# BENJAMIN FRANKLIN'S BIRTHPLACE { PAST }

**B**enjamin Franklin is more commonly associated with Philadelphia, but he is a son of Boston, born in a modest two-story wooden house at 17 Milk Street in 1706. The fifteenth child of Josiah Franklin, a candle and soap maker, and Josiah's second wife Abiah, he was baptized across the street at the Cedar Meeting House that previously stood on the site of the Old South Meeting House. Franklin's birthplace burned down in 1810.

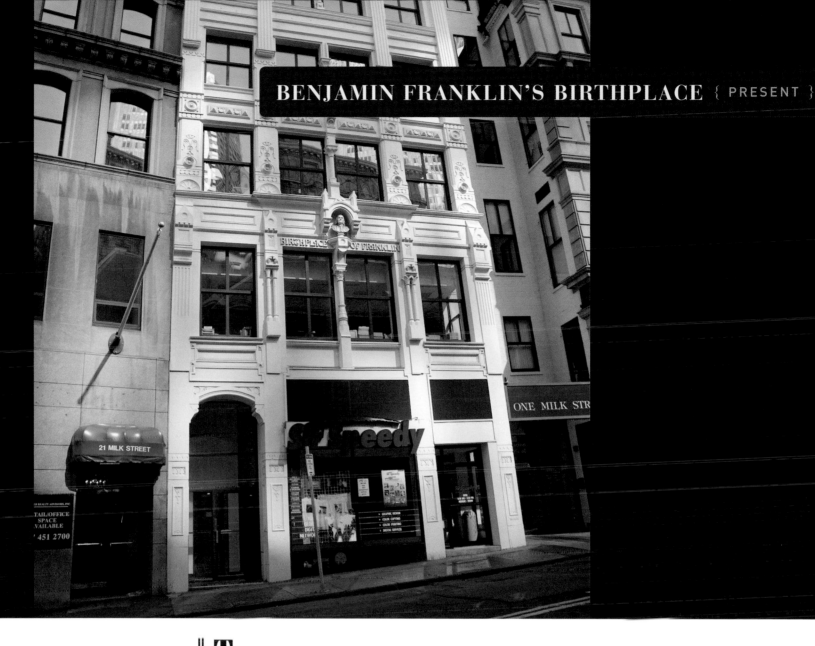

## BENJAMIN FRANKLIN'S BIRTHPLACE { PRESENT }

The building that currently occupies the location of Franklin's birthplace once housed the *Boston Post*, founded in 1831—the most popular daily newspaper in the city and New England for over a century until it closed in 1956. With its eclectic detailing, the building is considered a cast-iron masterpiece. After the Great Fire of 1872, iron-fronted buildings provided opportunity for considerable architectural elaboration at reasonable cost. Franklin's first home is marked by a bust and the words "Birthplace of Franklin" on the second-floor façade.

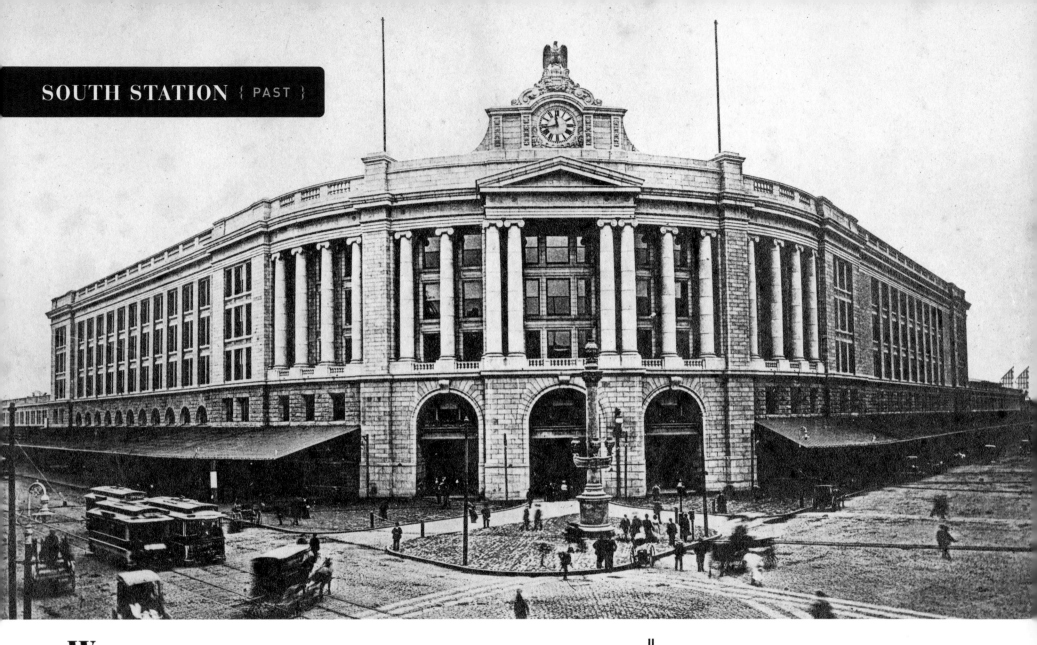

When it opened in 1899, the South Station was the largest train station in the world and the first to combine a terminal and an office building. The prototype of the "double-decker" terminal—with twenty-eight tracks on two floors—it consolidated five separate railroads, each with their own terminals, which had connected Boston to the south and west. It was a mammoth building: the paint used in a single coat would have covered 200 acres. By 1910, the station was the busiest in the country.

On the National Register of Historic Places, the South Station is the last remaining example of the Classical Revival style of railway architecture in Boston. The train shed was removed in 1930 and the building's wings demolished to build a postal annex and office building. But South Station has survived as a vital part of the city and region's transportation system. A $200 million "total makeover" in the 1980s and 1990s included the addition of a bus terminal above the tracks, an office complex, and a reinvigorated lobby with shops and amenities.

DINING SALOON.

Triangular trade between Boston, the West Indies, and Africa made Boston prosperous. Fish, livestock, hay, flour, and lumber was sent to the West Indies for sugar, coffee, cocoa, and molasses, which once made into rum, was sent to Africa in exchange for slaves to be sold in the Caribbean. India Wharf, 425-foot-long, with thirty-three five-story warehouses, was designed by Charles Bulfinch and built between 1803 and 1807 to accommodate this trade. Central Wharf, built a decade later with fifty-four brick stores and measuring 1300 feet in length, was the longest continuous block of warehouses in the country.

## CENTRAL AND INDIA WHARVES { PRESENT }

### LORE & LEGEND
One of the Aquarium's first residents, Myrtle, the green sea turtle, remains in the Giant Ocean Tank thirty years after her arrival.

In the mid-1800s, the port of Boston declined, as shipping shifted to New York City's deeper harbor and the 1868 extension of Atlantic Avenue split the Central Wharf. Twentieth-century urban renewal did the rest. A condominium and parking lot replaced the India Wharf. Only eight brick stores remain on Central Wharf. In 1969, the New England Aquarium was built on its eastern end, and a west wing was added in 1998.

The Custom House, built in 1847 in Greek Revival style, was one of the most expensive government buildings ever commissioned. Each Doric column was made from a single shaft of granite weighing 42 tons, and 3,000 piles were required to support the structure. In 1915, a 495-foot tower was built atop the classical temple to accommodate more revenue agents. As federal property, it was not bound by the city's height limitations of 125 feet, or approximately eleven stories, and for thirty years it dominated the city skyline.

The federal government moved out of the Custom House in 1987. After a $30-million-plus restoration, it opened in 1997 as the Marriott's Custom House, a luxury time-share hotel with eighty units. It is the anchor of the Custom House Historic District, which encompasses seventy buildings spread over 16 acres. With its many nineteenth-century mercantile buildings, the district gives the modern viewer a visible reminder of how important sea-borne trade was to the city's development.

Completed in 1892, this seven-story building of pink Worcester Quarry granite, with its rock-faced masonry, conical roof, and tiered arches, is a charming example of the Romanesque Revival style. It was built on land donated by the industry magnate Henry M. Whitney, who built the first electric streetcar in the Allston-Brighton neighborhood in 1888. The building housed the Boston Chamber of Commerce from 1892 to 1902 before becoming the home of the consolidated Boston Commercial and Boston Produce Exchanges.

# FLOUR AND GRAIN EXCHANGE BUILDING { PRESENT }

This fairy-tale castle of a building was restored in 1988 by its present owner, the real estate and investment firm Beal Companies. It now overlooks the Wharf District Parks, approximately five acres of parks and open spaces. These are being built as part of the 27-acre Rose Kennedy Greenway, the final piece of the Big Dig that removed the elevated Central Artery and will reconnect—through a mile and half of parks, pedestrian walkways, and cultural institutions—the waterfront and downtown Boston after a half century.

"The market of all markets," proclaimed one merchant at the August 26, 1826, opening of what two years before had been assailed as "Quincy's folly." Boston had become a city in 1822, and with 50,000 citizens, it had outgrown Faneuil Hall. Mayor Quincy's construction plan to fill in the waterfront, widen and add streets, and build three large granite buildings for stalls, stores, and warehouses, was the largest project yet undertaken in America. The 535-foot-long Greek Revival market revitalized the city life and commerce.

One hundred and fifty years later, to the day, Mayor Kevin White reopened a Quincy Market that not only revitalized Boston again, but also revolutionized how people thought about urban renewal nationwide. By 1900, the aging market, increasingly neglected and dilapidated, had lost almost all of its retail trade and was home to produce wholesalers, seed stores, and warehouses. Restored from 1974 to 1976, Quincy Market with its Colonnade of restaurants and the entire Faneuil Hall Marketplace area with its shops and exuberant street life have become a vibrant tourist attraction.

# Tasty Tales

## BOSTON BAKED BEANS

While Boston's early history may speak more to the mind and soul than to the stomach, the city has also contributed to the nation's menu and spiced up its culinary lore.

Not all the molasses brought to Boston from the West Indies in the "triangular trade" of the eighteenth and nineteenth centuries was made into rum and shipped to the west coast of Africa in exchange for slaves. There was still enough thick molasses for Puritan ladies to add to beans, mustard, and onions for their Sabbath meal. Before sundown on Saturday, they started the beans and cooked them slowly overnight. Later, bakers took over the task: they picked up the family bean pot on Saturday morning and returned it at the end of the day brimming with beans, along with bit of brown bread made with molasses. In the nineteenth century, Boston baked beans became a staple of the Irish immigrants' Saturday evening dinner.

## BOSTON CREAM PIE

Another busy workingman's wife may have been the creator of the state dessert, the calorie-busting Boston cream pie, which is no pie at all. Its origin, like the desert itself, is layered—not with cake, custard, and chocolate glaze, but with controversy. The Parker House claims it as the creation of the French chef that Henry Parker brought over to his kitchen in 1855 for the annual salary of $5,000—extravagant, when top chefs were making $8 a week.

Some food sleuths attribute the dessert instead to a German baker named Ward. James Beard skirts this Franco-Prussian skirmish and lays the origin to an earlier, anonymous New England cook who, tired of making two-crust fruit pies for her husband's breakfast, used a spare pie pan to try something easier and different.

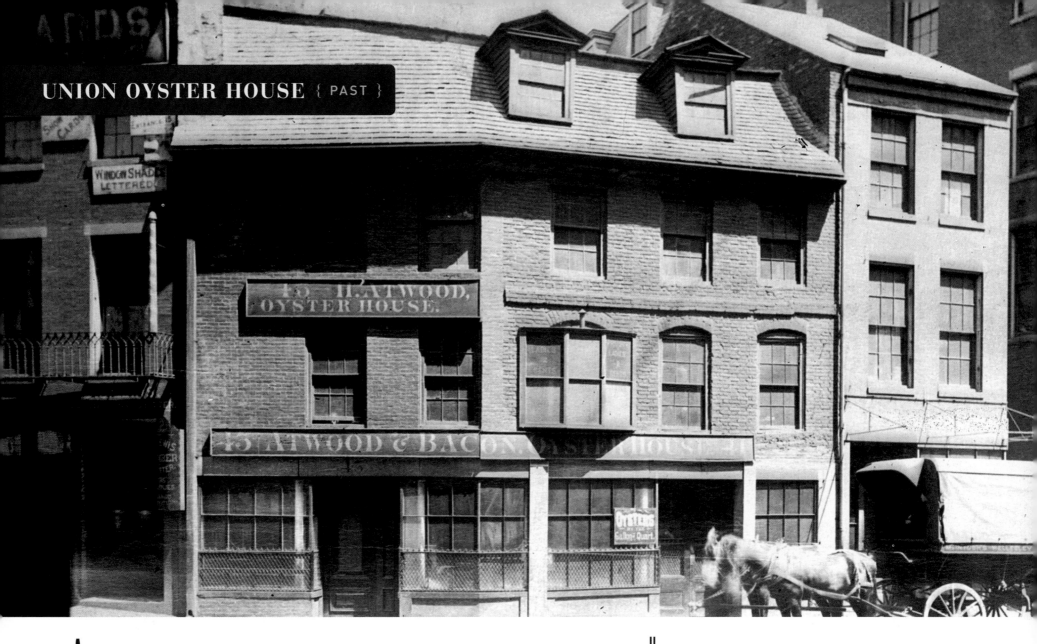

A dozen oysters for fifteen cents and apple pie for a nickel highlighted the Union Oyster House's inaugural menu. The restaurant occupied two brick houses dating from 1717 and 1724, which by 1771 were home to the radical newspaper the *Massachusetts Spy*, and four years later became the headquarters of the paymaster for the Continental Army. The restaurant opened in 1826 as part of a national craze for oysters. Daniel Webster, a regular, kept oratorically fit with thirty-six oysters washed down with a half-dozen tumblers of brandy and water.

Listed as a National Historical Landmark in 2003, the Union Oyster House is the country's oldest restaurant in continuous operation, and it has had only three families as owners in all these years. Diners can still slurp oysters at the original U-shaped mahogany bar and in the booths on the first floor, or they can sit upstairs in booth 18, which was JFK's favorite and is marked with a bronze plaque.

## BLACKSTONE STREET { PAST }

Named after the city's first permanent resident, Reverend William Blackstone, this street and the surrounding alleys and lanes were, in the late nineteenth century, still a vibrant reminder of the city's colonial architectural past. Nearby, embedded in a building on Marshall Street, is the 1737 Boston Stone, the center of town from which colonial surveyors measured distance from the city. The North End was a microcosm of the city's changing population—from Yankee to heavily Irish, then Jewish, and finally the heart of the city's Italian community.

The Central Artery, a roadway completed in 1959, engulfed one side of the street and separated the North End and the waterfront from the rest of Boston. This elevated eyesore was torn down and replaced by a tunnel as part of the Big Dig forty-four years later, but irreparable damage had been done to the neighborhood's social fabric. Now part of the Blackstone Block Historic District, Blackstone Street holds a weekend open-air market, but it is a faint echo of the previous centuries' vibrant street life.

The Congregationalist New North Church was built in 1714, enlarged in 1730, and redesigned in 1804 by Charles Bulfinch. In 1814, it became the Second Unitarian Church, but with the influx of Irish immigrants, young married families soon moved out of the neighborhood and didn't think it genteel to worship in the North End. The Roman Catholic diocese bought the church in 1862 and renamed it St. Stephen's. In the 1870s, the building was raised six and a half feet to add another level to accommodate the growing numbers of Irish Catholics in the area.

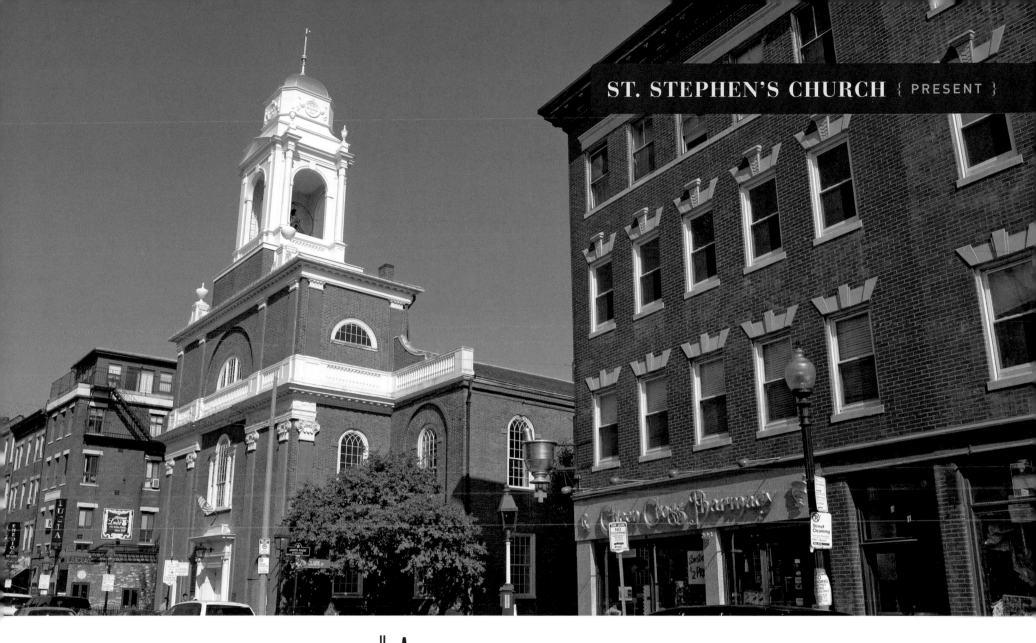

After the interior was damaged by fires in 1897 and 1929, the church deteriorated and was closed for a yearlong restoration in 1964. The most extensive restoration ever undertaken by the Archdiocese won the Boston Society of Architects Award for Historic Preservation and returned the church to Bulfinch's original design. The church was lowered, doorways and windows replaced or bricked over, chandeliers duplicated, and the cupola dismantled and reconstructed. Now it is the only surviving Bulfinch church in Boston.

PAUL REVERE HOUSE { PAST }

Built in 1680, this structure is considered the oldest surviving house in downtown Boston. In 1770, Paul Revere moved into the house with his wife and five children. He remarried after being widowed three years later, and continued living here until 1780. Revere set out from this house on his famous ride, though a British patrol intercepted him before he got to Concord. He rented out the house and eventually sold it in 1800. It went through many incarnations over the next century—candy factory, cigar factory, grocery store, and tenement.

PAUL REVERE HOUSE { PRESENT }

Immigrants flooded the North End in the nineteenth century, and the house fell into disrepair. John Phillips Reynolds Jr., a fourth-generation descendant of Paul Revere, formed the Paul Revere Memorial Association in 1905, and the home was opened to the public in April 1908 as one of the first historic house museums in the country. However, in restoring the house to its original "folk Gothic" style with a steep gabled roof, clapboard siding, and leaded windows, they removed the third floor that had been there during Revere's residence.

Made famous by Longfellow's "one if by land, two if by sea," the Old North Church, built in 1723, is the oldest surviving church building in Boston. It took special courage for sexton Robert Newman to hang the lanterns, as the majority of the Anglican congregation was loyal to the King. The 175-foot, three-tiered steeple Newman climbed was toppled by an 1804 storm and rebuilt from a Bulfinch drawing, but toppled again in 1954. The current steeple is a copy of the 1740 original with the original weathervane.

## LORE & LEGEND

The official name of the Old North Church is Christ Church in the City of Boston. Its nickname leads to confusion with the Old North Meeting House, which was also located in Boston during the Revolution.

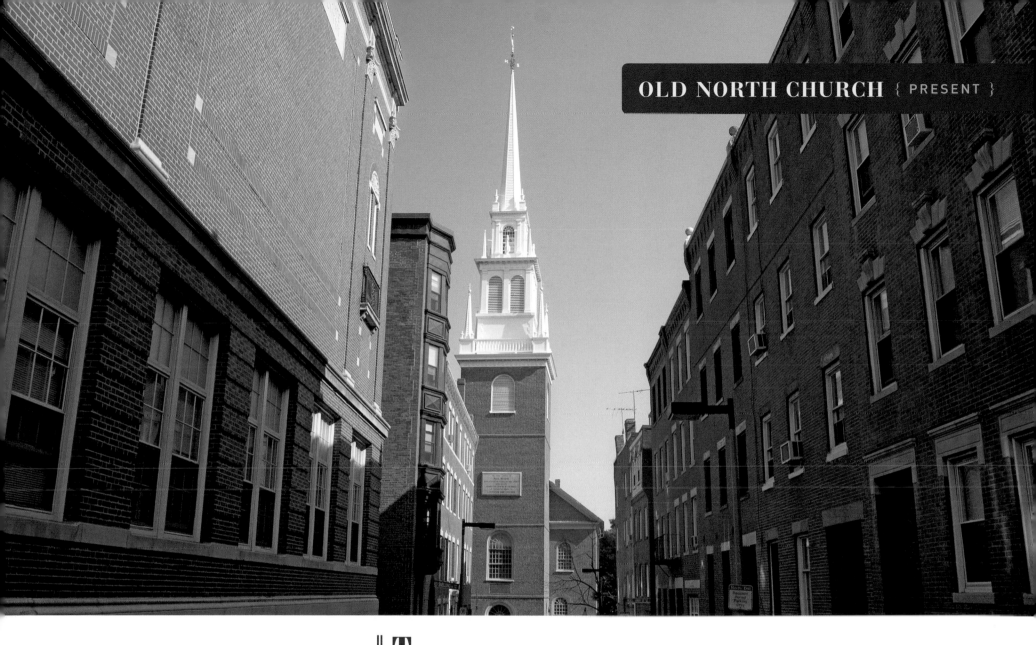

The North End has undergone many changes since 1775, but the church remains, protected by its poetically enhanced history. The window through which Newman escaped was bricked up in 1815, but rediscovered during a 1989 restoration. At the bicentennial celebration of the midnight ride, President Gerald Ford lit a third lantern that sits in "Newman's Window." This active Episcopal church's bells, which are still rung today, date from 1744, making them the oldest church bells in America. On Friday nights from July to October, Paul Revere comes alive in the one-man show, "Paul Revere Tonight!"

The 221-foot-high, 6700-ton granite obelisk commemorates the deadliest battle of the Revolutionary War, fought June 17, 1775, here on Breed's Hill—not on Bunker's Hill a half-mile away. Even in defeat, the outnumbered and ill-equipped colonial troops inflicted twice as many casualties on the British redcoats. The Marquis de Lafayette laid the cornerstone in 1825, and Daniel Webster spoke both then and at the 1843 dedication.

## LORE & LEGEND

In true American philanthropic fashion, a female-led, week-long cake and cookie sale in 1840 raised over $30,000, almost one-fifth of the total monument cost.

## BUNKER HILL MONUMENT { PRESENT }

I n 1919, beset by continuing financial problems, the bankrupt Bunker Hill Memorial Association turned the monument over to the city, which in turn transferred the monument to the National Park Service during the 1976 American Bicentennial for financial reasons. The monument reopened in April 2007 after an almost year-long renovation. In the adjacent marble lodge built at the turn of the twentieth century, park rangers tell visitors the story of the battle through dioramas.

Launched in Boston in 1797, "Old Ironsides" got its name during the War of 1812, when cannonballs from the HMS *Guerriere* bounced off its thick wooden hull as if it was made of iron. Oliver Wendell Holmes' 1830 poem spurred popular protest and saved the ship from scrap. Decommissioned in 1882, she was a receiving ship for recruits in Portsmouth before returning to Boston in 1897 for her centennial. In 1931, she was recommissioned.

## LORE & LEGEND

The USS *Constitution* was saved from target practice in 1905 by public sentiment, and again in 1925 by a schoolchildren's pennies campaign.

Berthed at the Charlestown Navy Yard, the ship is the oldest commissioned warship in the world. In its fighting days, it had a crew of 450, while now only 50 to 80 sailors are onboard. It was most recently restored in 1997 to celebrate the two hundredth anniversary of its launching, and in July 1997 it sailed under its own power for the first time in 116 years. The ship now sails the harbor in the summer, and visitors can attend morning and evening colors complete with cannon fire.

## BOSTON GARDEN { PAST }

On November 14, 1928, President Calvin Coolidge flipped a switch in the White House to turn on the lights at Boston Garden. For sixty-seven years, it was the city's premier site for sports and popular entertainment. The Boston Celtics won sixteen NBA championships here, the Boston Bruins won five Stanley Cups, and the Grateful Dead performed twenty-four times. By the time the Bruins played their final game here in 1995, power failures had interrupted several hockey matches, and it was rumored that escaped circus monkeys roamed the rafters.

In 1995, the Fleet Center replaced the Garden above North Station. Pieces from the Garden's fabled parquet basketball floor were integrated with the new floor, while other pieces were sold as souvenirs along with the seats from the old Garden. TD Banknorth bought the naming rights for the arena in 2005 and now calls the arena the TD Banknorth Garden in honor of the old Garden. The magic of the name has not yet rubbed off on either the Celtics or Bruins.

# The Brawn of Boston

## Who says Boston is only a city of the mind?

Every year a half million people line the streets to cheer on the thousands running in the Boston Marathon. Sixteen NBA Championship banners once hung above the Boston Garden's parquet floor (and now grace the TD Banknorth Garden). The Stanley Cup was hoisted five times high above the Garden's ice. And more than three million fans lined the streets on October 30, 2004, to chant the names of Pedro, Papi, and the other victorious Sox. From Cy Young to Bobby Orr and Larry Bird, Boston has long been a sports town, its diamonds, courts, rinks, and fields star-studded with history.

There was never any "Curse of the Bambino," just a bad bounce or two or three that kept the Red Sox from winning the World Series for eighty-six years. These hiccups on the way to success have often garnered more ink and memories than the highlights of Boston's baseball history:

- The first World Series game was played at the Huntington Avenue Grounds between the Boston Americans and the Pittsburg Pirates on October 1, 1903. Though the Americans lost the first game, Boston won the first World Series and four more before the ill-fated trade of Babe Ruth to the New York Yankees in 1920.

- Cy Young threw the first perfect game in the modern era on May 5, 1904, at the Huntington Avenue Grounds, an immense playing field whose center field was 635 feet deep.

- Ted Williams batted .406 in 1941—the last player to hit over .400—and his dramatic home run in his last time at bat in 1960 was icing on the cake.

- The Red Sox became the only team in baseball ever to win a seven-game series after falling behind three games to none when they defeated their archrival Yankees in the 2004 American League Championship.

And, of course, there is the continued presence of Fenway Park, opened in 1912—the oldest major league ballpark still in operation.

Probably no team in professional sports can match the successful run of the Boston Celtics in the late 50s through the mid-70s. Under coach Red Auerbach, the Boston Celtics won eight straight NBA championships and nine in eleven years. In all, they have won sixteen championships, more than any other NBA team. The Celtics under Auerbach were the first NBA team to draft an African-American player and the first to put five African-Americans on the court at the same time. Bill Russell, Bob Cousy, Jo Jo White, Tom Heinsohn, Tom Sanders, Sam Jones, John Havlicek, Kevin McHale, Robert Parish, and Larry Bird are among the stars that made history on the famous parquet floor of the now demolished Boston Garden.

As the Celtics' fortunes have waned in recent years, Boston's football fortunes have risen. The Boston Patriots played in the first regular season game of the newly founded American Football League on September 9, 1960. After the merger of the two leagues in 1970, the team was renamed the New England Patriots and moved twenty-four miles south to Foxborough. Between 2001 and 2004, they became only the second team to win three Super Bowls in a row. Like the Red Sox, the Pats are a Boston team with a New England following, regardless of where they play their home games.

From the Quincy quarries came granite not only to build the Bunker Hill Monument and Quincy Market, but also the Charles Street Jail, completed in 1851 and one of the finest examples of the "Boston Granite School." A seminal design in correctional architecture, it rejected the Quaker-inspired Pennsylvania System of continuous solitary confinement with individual cells opening into individual exercise yards. The new design embodied the Auburn Plan, with space for communal work and exercise performed in silence, and solitary confinement at night.

The last inmates were removed from the jail in 1991. Its neighbor, Massachusetts General Hospital, bought the property for development. One wing of the jail was reconstructed as the entrance to the Yawkey Center for Outpatient Care. The central rotunda and three other wings are part of a three-hundred-room luxury hotel that opened in the summer of 2007. Historic preservation rules required that some jail cells be retained and bars kept on some windows. Elsewhere irony replaced iron bars: the hotel is called the Liberty Hotel.

The Colonial, one of the first theaters built in the theater district that arose at the southern end of Tremont Street, opened on December 20, 1900. The first show was *Ben-Hur*, complete with a chariot race featuring live horses running on a treadmill. Though it seated 1,700 people, it was praised for its intimacy, sight lines, and excellent acoustics—Thomas Edison was a consultant. When Boston was a "tryout town" for Broadway, Ethel Barrymore, Helen Hayes, Paul Robeson, Bob Hope, and Katherine Hepburn were among the galaxy of stars that graced its boards.

The Colonial remains the oldest surviving theater in Boston. Modest on the outside, its opulent interior got a $750,000 renovation in 1960. Its Italian marble walls, frescoes, mosaic floor, giant mirrors, bronze staircases, chandeliers, gilt ornamentation, and allegorical artwork have occasioned comparisons to Pompeii, the Louvre, and Fontainebleau. Now the theatrical flow has reversed, and shows come here after their Broadway success.

Built in 1828, the Tremont House was the city's first modern hotel. Instead of large rooms with several beds as in a colonial inn, Tremont House had 170 rooms, all with locks, a washbasin and pitcher, a lamp, and a free cake of soap. Likely the most satisfying "first" the hotel offered was indoor plumbing. Guests could bathe in bathtubs in the basement and relieve themselves in eight water closets on the ground floor.

## LORE & LEGEND

Tremont House catered to presidents and dignitaries, among them Andrew Jackson, Charles Dickens, Alexis de Tocqueville, and William Makepeace Thackeray.

The Tremont House was demolished in 1894 to 1895, and an office building now sits on the site where indoor plumbing once amazed its guests. The hotel's contemporary rival, the Parker House, is still in operation nearby on School Street.

**O**ne of the jewels of the Emerald Necklace—a 7-mile, 2,000-acre string of ponds and parks linked by a series of parkways designed by Frederick Law Olmstead between 1878 and 1892— the Arnold Arboretum was established in 1872 with a bequest of 137 acres to Harvard. Charles Sprague Sargent, the Arboretum's guiding spirit and director for its first fifty years, imagined the Arboretum serving the "scientific and the picturesque"—the scholar and the everyday visitor who could gain pleasure and knowledge "without even leaving his carriage."

Now almost double its original acreage with 265 acres, the Arboretum has a living collection of over 7,000 plants representing over 4,500 botanical and horticultural groups, with special focus on the woody species of North America and eastern Asia. The naturalistic style and plant arrangement envisioned by Sargent and Olmstead remains. But even nature can benefit from technology. Complete records of every plant are stored in a computerized database, linked to a computerized mapping program that locates each plant by mobile GPS equipment.

The last and largest jewel of Olmstead's Emerald Necklace, this 520-acre "country park" was intended to recreate the feel of the New England countryside. Like his Central Park and Prospect Park in New York, it was designed to be a healthy antidote to the deleterious effects of urban living. At its center was the Country Park intended for "passive recreation," and kept trim by grazing sheep. After Olmstead's death, forty lawn-tennis courts were put in the Ellicott Dale section of the Country Park for the more active set.

A zoo was added to the park in 1913 and a golf course in 1922, but demographic, economic, and social changes led to the park's decline and disrepair after WWII. Community activism and increased political support and funding led to the park's revitalization beginning in the 1980s. The golf course was reopened, the White Stadium was renovated, and the African Tropical Forest was added to the zoo. Revitalized, the park with its forests, picnic areas, playgrounds, and outcroppings of Roxbury puddingstone provide relaxation and active respite for the city that has grown up around it.

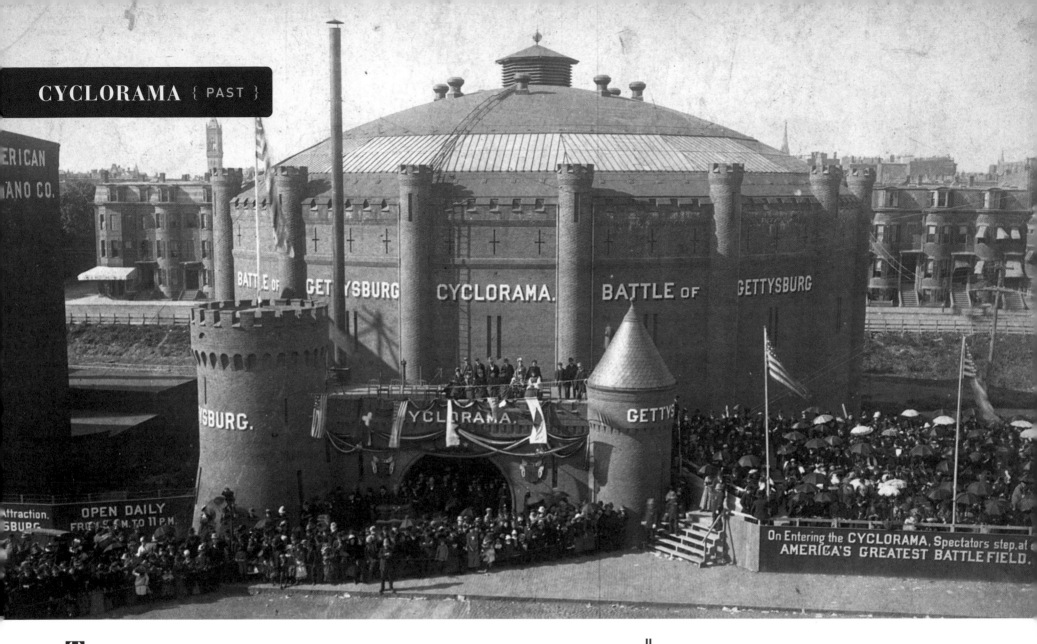

The Cyclorama was built in 1884, specifically to display the panoramic painting *The Battle of Gettysburg*. Pickett's confederate troops charged towards the viewers, who stood on a raised platform encircled by the painting, fifty feet high and four hundred feet in circumference. Other panoramic paintings followed over the next decade, including depictions of the Battle of Little Big Horn and volcanic eruptions. Lost for twenty years, the original painting was found in a vacant lot in Roxbury. Acquired by the National Park Service in 1924, it is now displayed at the Gettysburg National Military Park.

As the Casino Building and Boston Auditorium, the building hosted roller polo, bicycle races, dancers, and John L. Sullivan workouts until it became a garage in 1899. It has lost its turrets and battlements but has gained a 127-foot-diameter glass dome. Now on the National Register of Historic Places, the Cyclorama is the centerpiece of the Boston Center for the Arts. Its 23,000-square-foot rotunda hosts exhibitions, performances, and community events and houses local music and arts organizations, three small theaters, and a rehearsal studio.

Trinity Church, consecrated in 1877 in the newly created Back Bay, established the reputation of architect Henry Hobson Richardson. Richardson Romanesque, with its medieval-inspired rounded arches, massive towers, and rugged stone walls laid out in bands of contrasting color, is the only architectural style named after an American architect and spawned many copies in public buildings in the United States and abroad. Phillips Brooks, the church's charismatic minister, pushed for the move to Copley Square. After his death in 1893, the portico and front towers were added.

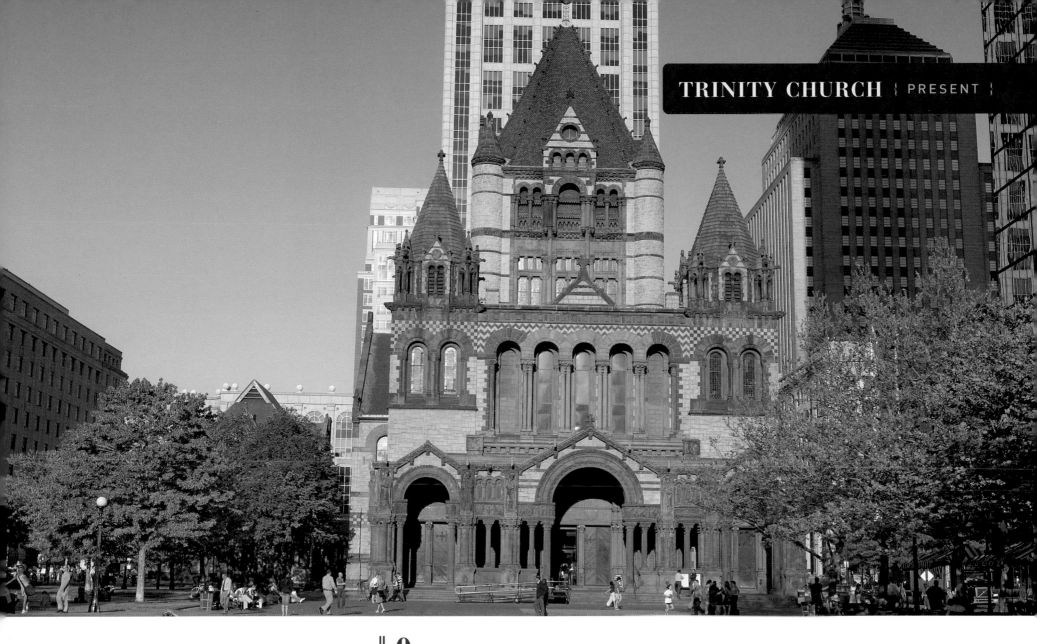

Over 100,000 people visit Trinity annually to admire the architecture and the art of this National Historic Landmark: stained glass windows by Edward Burne-Jones and William Morris, John La Farge's murals and revolutionary opalescent stained glass, and sculpture by Daniel Chester French and Augustus Saint-Gaudens. In 1885, architects voted Trinity Church the country's most important building, and today it is the only building from that original list still included in the American Institute of Architects' top ten. The sixty-story Hancock Tower, built in 1976, towers over but does not diminish Richardson's treasured legacy.

The third home of the Boston Public Library opened in Copley Square in 1895 in a Renaissance-inspired palazzo designed by the firm of McKim, Mead, and White. The Boston Public Library garners many firsts: the first large municipal library in American open to the public, the first public library to allow patrons to check out material, and the first to have a children's reading room. Decorated with marble, mosaic tiles, and murals by Pierre Puvis de Chavannes and John Singer Sargent, the library's cost was two and half times its original $1.16 million budget.

**W**ith a 1971 addition by Philip Johnson, the Boston Public Library is now the third largest library in the United States. "Free to All" can still be seen carved on the keystone of the central arch in the McKim building, and all adult residents of the Commonwealth have borrowing and research privileges. Among its holdings are two copies of the first book published in America, the Bowditch collection of rare mathematical works, and John Eliot's Indian Bible.

In 1879, Mary Baker Eddy held the first Church of Christ, Scientist services in her parlor. The Church expanded rapidly over the next decade, and in 1894 she built its Mother Church in Romanesque style, with room for 1,000 congregants. Soon more space was needed, but she wanted to preserve the original building, so an extension that dwarfed the original was built between 1904 and 1906. Its central dome incorporated elements of St. Peter's in London and the Duomo in Florence, and its auditorium, which was inspired by the Hagia Sophia, seated over 3,000.

# FIRST CHURCH OF CHRIST, SCIENTIST { PRESENT }

Based on an ambitious, comprehensive plan designed by I.M. Pei in 1963 for the Christian Science Center and surrounding area, the entire complex was redesigned from 1968 to 1973. Highlights of the fourteen-acre center are its 670-foot-long reflecting pool with circular fountain, a twenty-eight-story administration building and the elegant Colonnade Building with its 525 columns. The Library, originally built in 1934 for the Christian Science Monitor, houses the Mapparium—a 30-foot diameter stained-glass globe of the world in 1931 that visitors can walk through.

**B**oston financier Henry Lee Higginson founded the Boston Symphony Orchestra in 1880 and was its sole underwriter until 1918. When the BSO's Boston Music Hall home was threatened, Higginson purchased the land for a new hall that opened in 1900. Symphony Hall was the first auditorium designed according to scientifically based acoustical principles. Wallace Sabine, a Harvard physics professor, advised the architects McKim, Mead, and White on the shape of the hall; the slope of the walls, ceilings, and floors; building materials; and other elements for the best sound.

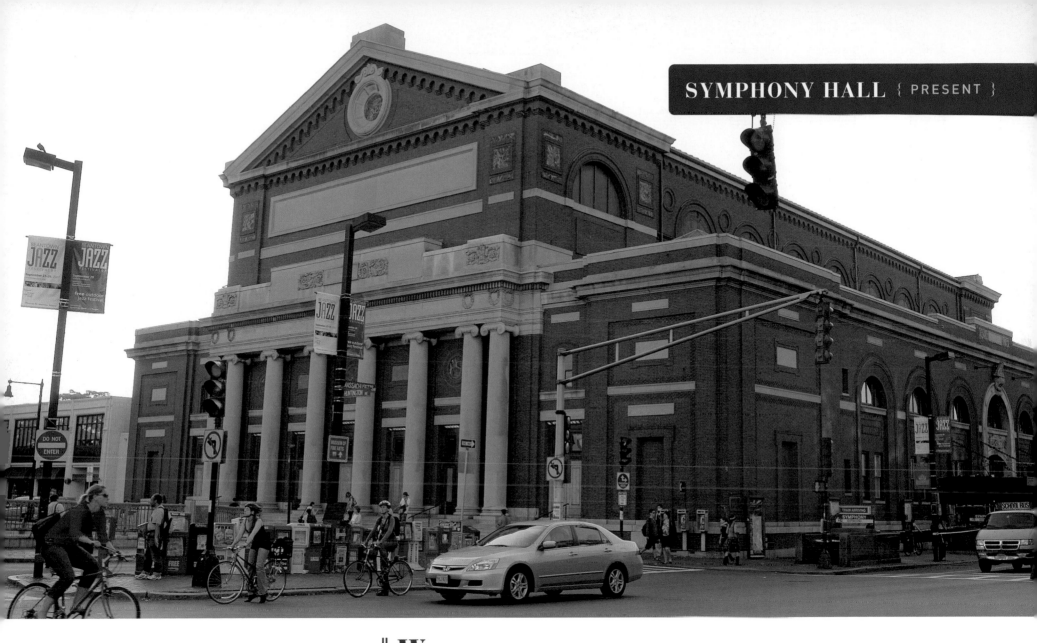

**W**hile Beethoven was chosen in 1900 as the only "great composer" to be inscribed on the plaques that ring the proscenium arch, the BSO and the Hall have been less conservative in its programming. Works by contemporary composers from Paul Hindemith to Bright Sheng have been premiered, Marian Anderson sang when banned elsewhere, and Isadora Duncan danced draped and barefoot. In 1919, the first flight across the Atlantic was told in slides and film, while years later, the Boston Pops under John Williams traveled to the distant galaxies of *Star Wars*.

# CHICKERING & SONS' FACTORY { PAST }

CHICKERING SONS' PIANO-FORTE MANUFACTORY.

In the nineteenth century, the South End was the center of Boston's piano industry. Completed in 1854, the Chickering factory spread over 5 acres and employed four hundred people. It was the largest factory in the nation and, some claim, the second largest building in the world. Jonas Chickering began the company in 1823, and in 1837 produced the first "scientifically" constructed grand piano. Chickering pianos won over two hundred first medals and awards and were owned by Abraham Lincoln, Franz Liszt, and Queen Victoria.

In 1974, the factory became the Piano Craft Guild Housing for Artists. It was the first mill-to-apartment conversion in the country and provided 174 apartments for visual artists, musicians, and dancers. Live-in studios were specifically designed for painters and the other artistic residents. The conversion won an American Institute of Architects First Honor Award in 1975 and is considered a key development in the movement to recycle old buildings.

# ISABELLA STEWART GARDNER MUSEUM { PAST }

Isabella Stewart Gardner, an heiress to two fortunes, lived as she pleased. She began collecting art in 1891 and by her death in 1924, had collected over 2,500 objects, including masterpieces by Vermeer, Botticelli, Raphael, Titian, and John Singer Sargent. She opened her Italian-inspired palace on the Fenway in 1903. She lived on the fourth floor, while the rooms below and the glass-covered interior courtyard blooming with seasonal flowers were open to the public twenty days a year.

Under the conditions of Gardner's will, the collection's arrangement was to remain as it did in the year of her death. If any piece was changed or sold, or any works were added, the entire collection would be sold for the benefit of Harvard. Now open throughout the year, her idiosyncratic arrangement remains the same except for thirteen works—including paintings by Vermeer, Rembrandt, Degas, and Monet—which were stolen on March 18, 1990. Despite an international investigation, the crime remains unsolved, and the paintings' frames are empty but still in place.

FENWAY PARK { PAST }

The Green Monster may be the most distinctive feature of any baseball park in America—turning potential homeruns into long singles. After Tom Yawkey bought the Red Sox in 1933, he spent two million dollars renovating the park built in 1912. The 37-foot-high, 240-foot-long wooden fence was replaced with sheet metal. In 1936, a 23-foot screen was added to save the windows on Lansdowne Street. The wall got its name in 1947 when its advertisements were painted over in the park's distinctive green.

Fenway Park, the oldest and smallest park in the majors, has a special charm: the manually operated scoreboard and the towering Green Monster that still frustrates batters. When the tin was replaced with fiberglass, the old pieces of the fence were cut up and sold to raise money for the Jimmy Fund, the official charity of the Red Sox. The "Curse of the Bambino" was broken with the team's 2004 World Series victory, and the Sox's on-the-field success has continued, resulting in sell-out crowds and another World Series victory in 2007.

# Boston on Film

*You've "visited" Boston if you've seen one of these movies or television shows filmed or set in the city:*

## Films:

- THE DEPARTED (2006)
- FEVER PITCH (2005)
- MYSTIC RIVER (2003)
- A CIVIL ACTION (1998)
- NEXT STOP WONDERLAND (1998)
- GOOD WILL HUNTING (1997)
- MRS. WINTERBOURNE (1996)
- WITH HONORS (1994)
- GLORY (1989)
- THE VERDICT (1982)

- THE FRIENDS OF EDDIE COYLE (1973)
- THE PAPER CHASE (1973)
- LOVE STORY (1970)
- THE BOSTON STRANGLER (1968)
- THE THOMAS CROWN AFFAIR (1968)
- THE LAST HURRAH (1958)
- JOHNNY TREMAIN (1957)

## TV Shows:

- THE SUITE LIFE OF ZACK & CODY (2005-PRESENT)

- BOSTON LEGAL (2004-PRESENT)
- CROSSING JORDAN (2001-2007)
- BOSTON PUBLIC (2000-2004)
- TWO GUYS, A GIRL AND A PIZZA PLACE (1998-2001)
- THE PRACTICE (1997-2004)
- ALLY MCBEAL (1997-2002)
- REAL WORLD: BOSTON (1997)
- SABRINA, THE TEENAGE WITCH (1996-2003)
- ST. ELSEWHERE (1982-1988)
- CHEERS (1982-1993)

Founded in 1636 (sixteen years after the Pilgrims landed), Harvard University is the oldest institution of higher learning in the United States. Massachusetts Hall, built in 1720, is the oldest standing Harvard building and housed soldiers of the Continental Army during the Revolutionary War. The Johnson Gate, built in 1898, is the most elaborate gate leading into Harvard Yard. It was designed by McKim, Mead, and White, who in 1899 were commissioned to design the fence that encloses the twenty-two-acre Harvard Yard.

**D**uring the school presidency of Charles W. Eliot, who from 1869 to 1909 transformed Harvard into a modern university, the schools of Business, Dental Medicine, and Arts and Sciences were established, the student body and faculty grew dramatically, the endowment increased ten-fold, and Radcliffe College was incorporated. (Though it took forty-nine years for women to be allowed in Harvard classrooms, and another twenty for them to receive Harvard diplomas before the full merger in 1999). Beginning with only nine, Harvard now has more than 18,000 undergraduate and graduate students.

At end of the Revolution, there was little besides Harvard College to attract travelers to Cambridge and few stores to serve the students. The name Harvard Square wasn't commonly used until the mid-nineteenth century. The Square changed with the arrival of the street railway in 1854 and the college's expansion under Eliot's presidency: enrollment went from 754 in 1870 to 3364 in 1909. Private dormitories in and near the Square, some with valet service and swimming pools, brought businesses—from brokerage firms to classy clothiers and dining rooms—to serve the students.

The subway, the college housing system, and the end of private dormitories led to commercial revitalization of the Square in the 1920s. Inexpensive restaurants and cafeterias, local stores catering to students, and the usual mix of urban shops remained through the mid-60s. Anti-war protests and the rise of youth culture brought students and youths not affiliated with Harvard into the Square for the first time. The markets, variety stores, and snack shops have given way to restaurants, banks, and national chains. The sleepy village square has become a "scene."

Between 1865 and 1868, Harvard alumni raised $370,000—one twelfth of the University's endowment—for a building to honor graduates who died for the Union. The Memorial Hall cornerstone was laid in 1870 and the building was completed in 1878. The polychromatic Gothic landmark consists of three main elements: the memorial transept with twenty-eight white marble tables bearing the names of the 136 dead, the 9,000-square-foot Alumni Hall with its soaring trusses and stained glass windows, and the 1166-seat Sanders Theatre, where commencements were held until 1922.

Alumni Hall, renovated and renamed Annenberg Hall, is once again a dining hall, now providing in Henry James's words, "laurels to the dead and dinners to the living." Its stained glass windows were cleaned, repaired, and re-leaded in the late 1980s and 90s, and are a sparkling panorama of artistic styles from late-nineteenth-century British design to the Opalescent Style of John LaFarge and Tiffany. In 1999, after extensive research, the tower that had burned down in 1956 was rebuilt to its 1878 form.

**W**ashington slept here. So did Martha. Built in 1759, the house was George Washington's headquarters during the Siege of Boston. Henry Wadsworth Longfellow first rented a room here in 1837, his first year as a professor of comparative literature at Harvard. When he married in 1843, his father-in-law bought the house as a wedding gift for the couple. Longfellow lived here until his death in 1882. During his life, it was a gathering place for social and cultural luminaries such as Dickens, Hawthorne, Emerson, Julia Ward Howe, and Charles Sumner.

Longfellow and his family had great respect for the house that "Washington has rendered sacred." Reproduced in his works and in magazines and postcards, the house was so famous that in the Colonial Revival Movement of the late nineteenth century, copies were built around the country. The last Longfellow to live here was Henry's grandson, who died in 1950. In 1972, the house became a National Historic Site. Its art, furniture and decorative objects reflect the poet's and his descendants' broad cultural interests.

JACOB BIGELOW STATUIT ET DEDICAVIT.

AMERICA CONSERVATA
AFRICA LIBERATA
POPULO JACRO ASSURGENTE
HEROUM SANGUINE FUSO

**M**t. Auburn Cemetery, founded in Cambridge in 1831, was the country's first garden cemetery. Inspired by Paris's Père-Lachaise Cemetery and England's picturesque gardens, classical monuments were spread around the initial 72 acres of landscaped hills, ponds, and woodlands. Mt. Auburn set the style for suburban cemeteries and began the public parks and gardens movement. An outdoor museum, an arboretum, and a public park, Mt. Auburn was for the living, not just the dead. A Who's Who of Boston luminaries rest here, from Longfellow to Mary Baker Eddy.

JACOB BIGELOW STATUIT ET DEDICAVIT

AMERICA CONSERVATA
AFRICA LIBERATA
POPULO MAGNO ASSURGENTE
HEROUM SANGUINE FUSO

A National Historic Landmark, the cemetery has over 30,000 monuments and memorial art covering many architectural styles, more than 5,500 labeled trees, shrubs, and plants, and landscaping styles ranging from Victorian plantings to contemporary gardens. Now more than 170 acres and with ten miles of roads and paths, the cemetery is a popular place for bird watchers and nature-lovers. Over 80,000 people are buried here. Some of the more memorable recent additions include Buckminster Fuller, Bernard Malamud, B.F. Skinner, and Justice Felix Frankfurter.

**WALDEN POND** { PAST }

Henry David Thoreau built a one-room house on land owned by his friend Emerson. He lived here for two years and two days starting on July 4, 1845. Walden Pond was surrounded by one of the few surviving woodlands in a heavily farmed area. Thoreau came "to front only the essential facts of life" but didn't live like a recluse. He visited friends, tended his vegetable garden, rowed his boat, observed nature, and wrote *A Week on the Concord and Merrimack Rivers* and the first of seven drafts of *Walden*.

Emerson sold the house to his gardener, who sold it to a farmer who moved it and used it to store grain before it was dismantled for scrap lumber and its roof used for an outbuilding. Walden Pond has been designated a National Historic Landmark and is part of the four-hundred-acre Walden Pond State Reservation where only 1,000 visitors are allowed daily, without dogs, bicycles, floats, or grills. Because of its special glacial origins, the 102-foot-deep glacial kettle-hole pond remains consistently pure and clear.

# Resources for Further Exploration

*Old Boston in Early Photographs, 1850-1918:*
*174 Prints from the Collection of the Bostonian Society.*
**Bergen, Philip.**
**Mineola, New York: Dover Publications, 1990.**
A visual portrait of the nineteenth-century city–its buildings and streets past and preserved. For an even more extensive look at the city's visual history, go to the Bostonian Society's online photo and postcard collection at http://rfi.bostonhistory.org/ and view its collection of 30,000 photographic prints, 1,200 stereographs, and 2,200 postcards.

*Cityscapes of Boston: An American City Through Time.*
**Campbell, Robert, and Peter Vanderwarker.**
**New York: Houghton Mifflin, 1992.**
Campbell, Pulitzer Prize winning architecture critic for the *Boston Globe*, documents the depredations of the automobile and architects in an unintended elegy for humane cityscapes lost under the guise of progress and renewal.

*Boston A to Z.*
**O'Connor, Thomas H.**
**Cambridge, Massachusetts: Harvard University Press, 2000.**
A renowned historian of Boston takes a personal and informal alphabetical journey through the city's history. Boston baked beans, cemeteries, the film *The Last Hurrah*, Sacco-Vanzetti, and the Molasses Explosion of 1919 are some of the engaging topics covered.

*Victorian Boston Today: Twelve Walking Tours.*
**Petronella, Mary M., ed.**
**Boston: Northeastern University Press, 2004.**
Drawing on cultural, social, and political history, the authors guide the reader down streets and past buildings on geographically and thematically organized tours that include Victorian women, Victorian authors, and ethnic diversity in the Victorian North End.

*Boston: A Topographical History. Third Enlarged Edition.*
**Whitehall, Walter Muir, and Lawrence W. Kennedy.**
**Cambridge, Massachusetts: Belknap Press of Harvard University Press, 2000.**
This revision of the 1959 original traces the development and transformation of the city's man-made landscape–its private and public buildings and neighborhood–from its founding to its late twentieth-century renewal.

*Boston Sites & Insights: An Essential Guide to Historic Landmarks In and Around Boston.*
**Wilson, Susan.**
**Boston: Beacon Press, 2004.**
A broad ranging tour of the city's cultural and historical landmarks, packed with legend, lore, and facts.

Boston History and Architecture.
**www.iboston.org**
Provides photos and detailed information about Boston's history, architecture, public art, and historic people, sites, and events. One of its links under "Historical Resources" even makes the history of the city's landfill an engaging, interactive topic.

Celebrate Boston.
**www.celebrateboston.com**
A wide-ranging site that includes current events and attractions, along with an eclectic selection of historical categories from famous Boston recipes, disasters, and crimes to the music and lyrics of patriotic songs and "obscure attractions and events" under "Strange Boston."

The Freedom Trail, Black Heritage Trail, and The Literary Trail of New England.
**www.thefreedomtrail.org**
**www.afroammuseum.org/trail.htm**
**www.literarytrailofgreaterboston.org**
These three sites give practical information on these popular tours as well as virtual tours with background information to prepare visitors for their walks through history.

Mass Moments.
**www.massmoments.org**
Users of this electronic almanac of Massachusetts history can listen to, read, and download lively information about Boston events and people, from the Great Boston Fire to the founding of Baker's Chocolate and the first World Series.

# Photo Credits

# Index